Because of Wi

MW01254341

Grades 4-6

Written by Nat Reed
Illustrated by Rick Ward

ISBN 1-55035-769-7
Copyright 2005
Revised January 2006
All Rights Reserved * Printed in Canada

Published in the United States by:
On the Mark Press
3909 Witmer Road PMB 175
Niagara Falls, New York
14305
www.onthemarkpress.com

Published in Canada by:
S&S Learning Materials
15 Dairy Avenue
Napanee, Ontario
K7R 1M4
www.sslearning.com

© On the Mark Press • S&S Learning Materials

OTM-14257 • SSN1-257 Because of Winn-Dixie

At A Glance

Learning Expectations	Chapters 1 & 2	Chapters 3 & 4	Chapters 5 - 7	Chapters 8 - 10	Chapters 11 & 12	Chapters 13 & 14	Chapters 15 - 17	Chapters 18 - 20	Chapters 21 & 22	Chapters 23 & 24	Chapters 25 & 26
Reading Comprehension											
• Identify and describe story elements	●	●	●	●	●	●	●	●	●	●	●
• Summarize events/details				●							
• Identify Descriptors	●										
Reasoning & Critical Thinking											
• Character traits, comparisons		●	●	●	●	●	●	●			●
• Use context cues - create analogies								●		●	
• Make inferences	●	●	●	●	●	●	●			●	●
• Determine the meaning of colloquialisms and other phrases	●				●	●	●	●	●	●	●
• Understand abstract concepts		●	●		●	●	●			●	
• Develop opinions and personal interpretations	●	●	●	●	●	●	●	●		●	●
• Write a letter to a newspaper								●			
• Conduct an interview								●			
• Develop research skills								●			
• Develop a brochure									●		
• Create a book cover											●
• Identify conflict											●
• Create a time line											●
• Create a map							●				
• Create a poem								●			
Vocabulary Development, Grammar & Word Use											
• Synonyms, antonyms and homonyms			●			●	●		●		
• Similes	●										
• Syllables			●				●				
• Compound Words						●					
• Descriptive words and phrases					●						
• Parts of speech				●							
• Dictionary and thesaurus skills	●		●		●		●	●	●		●
• Use words correctly in sentences	●			●	●						●
• Alphabetical order					●						
• Alliteration						●					
• Root words										●	
• Anagrams							●				

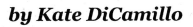

Because of Winn-Dixie
by Kate DiCamillo

Table of Contents

Because of Winn-Dixie
by Kate DiCamillo

Overall Expectations

The students will:

- develop their skills in reading, writing, listening and oral communication

- use good literature as a vehicle for developing skills required by curriculum expectations: reasoning and critical thinking, knowledge of language structure, vocabulary building, and use of conventions

- become meaningfully engaged in the drama of literature through a variety of types of questions and activities

- identify and describe elements of stories (i.e., plot, main idea, characters, setting)

- learn and review many skills in order to develop good reading habits

- provide clear answers to questions and well-constructed explanations

- organize and classify information to clarify thinking

- learn about the destructive nature of societal prejudice and stereotyping

- relate events and feelings found in the novel to their own lives and experiences

- appreciate the importance of friendship and loyalty in personal relationships

- learn the importance of dealing with adversity and developing perseverance in the face of adversity

- state their own interpretation of a written work, using evidence from the work and from their own knowledge and experience

Because of Winn-Dixie
by Kate DiCamillo

List of Skills

Vocabulary Development

1. Identifying / creating similes, alliteration
2. Locating descriptive words / phrases
3. Listing synonyms and antonyms
4. Using capitals and punctuation
5. Identifying syllables
6. Listing compound words
7. Using content clues: analogies
8. Identifying parts of speech
9. Determining alphabetical order
10. Determining meaning of colloquialisms

Setting Activities

1. Summarize the details of a setting
2. Identify hardships of moving to a new town
3. Create a time chart
4. Sketch a map of Naomi, Florida

Plot Activities

1. Complete a time line of events
2. Sequence main events
3. Determine the role of others in one's personal growth
4. Identify conflict in the story

Character Activities

1. Determine character traits
2. Compare two characters
3. Understand such concepts as *perseverance*, *self-respect,* and *stereotypes*
4. Relating personal experiences

Creative and Critical Thinking

1. Research epilepsy
2. Research elements from the American Civil War
3. Write a letter to a local newspaper
4. Conduct an interview
5. Decision-making exercise
6. Write a description of personal feelings

Art Activities

1. Design a brochure advertising a party
2. Design a cover for the novel

Because of Winn-Dixie

by Kate DiCamillo

Teacher Suggestions

This resource may be used in a variety of ways:

1. The student booklet focuses, for the most part, on one chapter of the novel at a time. Each of these sections contains the following activities:

   a) **Before you read the chapter** (reasoning and critical thinking skills)
   b) **Vocabulary building** (dictionary and thesaurus skills)
   c) **Questions on the chapter** (reading comprehension skills)
   d) **Language activities** (grammar, punctuation, word structure and extension activities)

2. Students may read the novel at their own speed and then select, or be assigned, a variety of questions and activities.

3. **Bulletin Board and Interest Center Ideas:** Themes might include Florida, dogs, pet shops, the American Civil War, thunderstorms, types of candies (i.e., lozenges).

4. **Pre-Reading Activities:** *Because of Winn-Dixie* may also be used in conjunction with themes of self-esteem, perseverance, family values, pet care, societal prejudice (the elderly), the danger of making lasting first impressions, and losing a parent.

5. **Independent Reading Approach:** Students who are able to work independently may attempt to complete the assignments in a self-directed manner. Initially these students should participate in the pre-reading activities with the rest of the class. Students should familiarize themselves with the reproducible student booklet. Completed work sheets should be submitted so that the teacher may note how quickly and accurately the students are working. Students may be brought together periodically to discuss issues in specific sections of the novel.

6. **Fine Art Activities:** Students may integrate such topics as the American Civil War (issues such as self-sacrifice), dogs and other pets, thunderstorms, the types of buildings found in the novel (i.e., haunted house, trailer, petshop). Students may also wish to plan their own party around a theme, making sure they include all the important details in organizing such an event.

7. Encourage the students to keep a reading log in which they record their reading each day and their thoughts about the passage.

8. Students should keep all their work together in one place. A portfolio cover is provided for this reason (see p. 10).

9. Students should not be expected to complete all activities. Teachers should allow choice and in some cases match the activity to the student's ability.

10. Students should keep track (in their portfolio) of the activities they complete.

Synopsis

Ten-year-old India Opal Buloni recounts her first summer in the town of Naomi, Florida, and all the good things that happen to her because of her big, ugly dog Winn-Dixie.

Opal finds moving to Naomi, Florida with her preacher father very difficult, but when she adopts a stray dog she finds at the local supermarket, her life takes a dramatic turn for the better. With the help of her new animal friend, Winn-Dixie, Opal makes a number of new, fascinating friends, and manages to get her reluctant father to finally open up about her long-absent mother. Opal's new friends include the town "witch", Gloria Dump, who becomes a wise, mother-figure to Opal. She also befriends the town librarian, Franny Block, who shares with Opal some of the exciting stories from her family's past as well as Littmus Lozenge candies (that taste like rootbeer and strawberry, mixed with a special ingredient – sorrow). Opal also makes friends with Otis, the pet shop owner, whose guitar playing touches both Opal and all of the animals in the shop. Opal grows to appreciate all of the wonderful things in her life, makes friends with other children she thought would be impossible to like, and also begins to realize that her mother is never coming back.

Because of Winn-Dixie
by Kate DiCamillo

Author Biography

Kate DiCamillo

Kate DiCamillo was born in Philadelphia, Pennsylvania and moved with her family to Florida when she was five years old. Kate DiCamillo has a Bachelor's of Art degree in English but didn't start writing children's books until she got a job at a book warehouse on the children's floor. There she started reading some of the books, and was so impressed that she decided to try her hand at it. Kate has lived in Minneapolis, Minnesota since her twenties, where she writes and works full time in a used bookstore. *Because of Winn-Dixie* was her first novel. She describes the book as "a hymn of praise to dogs, friendship, and the South." The novel won a number of awards including a *Newbery Honor*. Kate DiCamillo's second novel, *The Tiger Rising*, was a National *Book Award finalist, and her third novel, The Tale of Despereaux: Being the Story of a Mouse, A* Princess, Some Soup, and a Spool of Thread earned her the coveted 2004 Newbery Medal. Kate says that the biggest thrill in having a book published is to get a letter from a child saying, 'I loved your book. Will you write me another one?'

Because of Winn-Dixie
by Kate DiCamillo

Student Checklist

Name: _____

Assignment	Grade/Level	Comments

Because of Winn-Dixie
by Kate DiCamillo

Name: _____

Because of Winn-Dixie
by Kate DiCamillo

Chapters One and Two

Before you read the chapters:

The novel's main character is named **India Opal Buloni**. Later in the novel Opal admits that she was often teased because of her surname. Explain why you think this would be the case.

_____

_____

Define two meanings of the word **baloney** (use a dictionary if necessary).

_____

_____

What is another way of spelling **baloney**?_____

Have you ever moved to a new town or to a new home across town? Describe the **difficulties** that such a move might cause.

_____

_____

Vocabulary:

Choose a word from the list to complete each sentence.

concerned	display	hollered	cashier	immediately
distracted	sermon	admit	exceptions	specific

1. If you want something right away, ask for it to be done _____.

2. When people lose their concentration, they are said to be _____.

3. The clergyman delivered an interesting _____ at church on Sunday.

4. The _____ mother had a worried look on her face.

5. The department store put a variety of sporting goods on _____.

6. There were no _____ to the rules of the school.

Because of Winn-Dixie
by Kate DiCamillo

7. A clerk working behind the counter is called a _____.

8. To confess to a crime is to _____ one's guilt.

9. When planning a trip, one should be _____ about the route and destination.

10. Johnny's mother _____ at him to come for supper.

Questions

1. The dog in chapter one is quite unique in appearance. Check the following descriptors that apply to the dog.

   ☐ big ☐ tailless ☐ tongue hanging out
   ☐ wagging tail ☐ skinny ☐ bald patches
   ☐ female ☐ ugly

2. Why did the dog always appear to be smiling?

   _____

3. What three things was Opal supposed to bring back from the grocery store?

   _____

4. What did she bring home instead?

   _____

5. What was Opal afraid might happen if the manager called the pound?

   _____

6. What made Opal think that the dog did not belong to anyone?

   _____

7. Describe the setting of the story. Be specific (example: the time of year, place).

   _____

Because of Winn-Dixie

by Kate DiCamillo

8. What did Opal's dad do for a living before becoming a preacher? What would be the responsibilities of such an occupation?

   _____

9. What three things tended to distract the preacher?

   _____

10. Why do you think the preacher allowed Opal to keep the dog?

   _____

Language Activities

1. The author seems to enjoy using **similes** to describe different things. (A **simile** is a comparison using the words **like** or **as**.) Examples from the story include:

   ". . . he looked like a big piece of old brown carpet that had been left out in the rain."

   ". . . their taillights glowed red, like mean eyes staring at us."

   Use similes to compare the following:

   a) The sound of a small dog barking - _____

   b) The frigid temperature of winter - _____

   c) The threats of a schoolyard bully - _____

2. Explain what you think Opal meant by the following statement: **"It's hard not to immediately fall in love with a dog who has a good sense of humor."** Do you think she is right? Explain.

   _____

   _____

   _____

   _____

Because of Winn-Dixie
by Kate DiCamillo

Chapters Three and Four

Before you read the chapters:

Having a pet usually means additional **responsibilities**. What might these include for Opal?

_____

_____

Pets (especially dogs) often have very human-like characteristics (example: acting ashamed when being scolded). Think of a couple of other **human-like traits** you have seen in pets like Winn-Dixie.

_____

_____

Vocabulary:

Draw a straight line to connect the vocabulary word to its definition. Remember to use a straight edge (like a ruler).

1.	insult	a)	formation of stars
2.	intended	b)	to learn by heart
3.	orphan	c)	special ability
4.	handsome	d)	a gentle push
5.	constellation	e)	to treat rudely
6.	memorize	f)	instrument used to see very small things
7.	recognize	g)	good-looking
8.	microscope	h)	meant to
9.	talent	i)	child without parents
10.	nudge	j)	to show awareness

Because of Winn-Dixie
by Kate DiCamillo

Questions

1. How could Opal tell Winn-Dixie did not like being bathed?

   _____

2. How did Opal know that her father was still in love with her mother?

   _____

3. Why did Opal not have any friends?

   _____

4. Why do you think Opal had been thinking of her mother since moving from Watley?

   _____

5. Why didn't Opal discuss her mother with the preacher?

   _____

6. Why did Opal finally give up trying to clean Winn-Dixie's teeth?

   _____

Language Activities

1. In chapter four, the preacher tells Opal **ten interesting things about her mother**. List **ten** important things about **yourself** that you feel are worth sharing with your friends. Try to include a couple of things that they might not know about you.

   _____

   _____

   _____

2. The preacher reveals a **sense of humor** in chapter four by saying that Opal's mother was such a poor cook she "burned everything, including water." Think of another humorous way to describe someone's poor cooking ability.

   _____

   _____

   _____

Because of Winn-Dixie

by Kate DiCamillo

Chapter Five

Before you read the chapter:

Opal's father, the preacher, has a normal occupation but chooses to do his job **differently** than a lot of ministers. What might be good about this? How might this cause problems?

_____

_____

Do you think it would be a good idea to take a new dog to **obedience school**? Explain your answer.

_____

_____

Vocabulary:

Use a dictionary to find out the meaning of the following words.

1. congregation - _____

2. ought - _____

3. ignore - _____

4. exact - _____

5. except - _____

6. potluck - _____

7. applaud - _____

Because of Winn-Dixie

by Kate DiCamillo

Questions

1. Why couldn't Winn-Dixie be left alone?

   _____

2. List one thing that was different about the Open Arms Baptist Church.

   _____

3. Why did Opal have to go and get Winn-Dixie during the church service?

   _____

4. Describe how Winn-Dixie created a disturbance once he was inside the church.

   _____

5. The preacher once again reveals his sense of humor. Explain.

   _____

6. Why did Opal think that the other children would not want to be her friend?

   _____

Language Activity

Choose **ten** words from chapter five with **two or more syllables**. Indicate the syllables by drawing a line between the syllables. (**Example: Nord/ley**.)

_____   _____

_____   _____

_____   _____

_____   _____

_____   _____

Because of Winn-Dixie
by Kate DiCamillo

Chapters Six and Seven

Before you read the chapters:

The setting of chapters six and seven is in the local library. There Opal meets a fascinating woman, Franny Block, who opens Opal's eyes to the world of good literature. What is the best book you have ever read? What did you like best about it?

_____

_____

What animal would you least like to meet alone on a dark night? Why?

_____

_____

Vocabulary:

Synonyms are words with **similar meanings**. Using the context of the sentences below, choose the **best** synonym for the **underlined** word in each sentence. If you are unsure, check the dictionary definition.

1. Old Mr. Jameson had some very **peculiar** habits.

   a) cruel   **b)** unusual   **c)** expensive   **d)** old-fashioned

2. Susan was not **aware** of the fact that her cat was lost.

   a) conscious   **b)** happy   **c)** bragging   **d)** telling everybody

3. The bank teller was not **properly** prepared for the large number of customer complaints.

   a) light-heartedly   **b)** formally   **c)** unfortunately   **d)** correctly

4. The **hind** legs of the mare were injured when she tumbled.

   a) crippled   **b)** front   **c)** rear   **d)** muscular

5. Rosemary decided to **select** a bracelet for her birthday from the cabinet.

   a) choose   **b)** return   **c)** pay for   **d)** ignore

Because of Winn-Dixie
by Kate DiCamillo

6. Charles was extremely **prideful** of his accomplishments.

    a) gracious   **b)** unaware   **c)** arrogant   **d)** ignorant

7. The queen hadn't **intended** to be so cruel to the maid.

    a) been paid   **b)** meant   **c)** shown-off   **d)** told everyone

Questions

1. What was it that scared Miss Franny when Opal visited her at the library?

_____

2. Of what unpleasant experience did this remind Miss Franny?

_____

3. What birthday present did Miss Franny ask for when she was about Opal's age?

_____

4. What book did Miss Franny throw at the bear?

_____

5. What kind of personality did Amanda Wilkinson have? Give proof from the novel.

_____

Language Activity

Nicknames can be a lot of fun, but they may also be hurtful putdowns. In these chapters, **Franny Block refers to herself as "little-miss-know-it-all"** and **"little-miss-smarty-pants"**. Later, Opal refers to another girl as **"old pinch-faced Amanda Wilkinson"**.

From your own personal experience, give three examples of nicknames that you would not mind having (**Example: Ace**):

_____   _____   _____

Now give three examples of nicknames that are hurtful putdowns:

_____   _____   _____

Because of Winn-Dixie
by Kate DiCamillo

Chapter Eight

Before you read the chapter:

Have you ever **saved up** your money for something you wanted to buy? If so, write about your experience.

_____

_____

What do you like best about visiting a **pet shop**? If you owned a pet shop, what animals would you be sure to include?

_____

_____

What would be some **challenges** of being a pet shop owner?

_____

_____

Vocabulary:

Write a sentence using the following words. Make sure that the meaning of each word is clear in your sentence.

absolutely - _____

expensive - _____

irritating - _____

furious - _____

situation - _____

combination - _____

installment - _____

ponytail - _____

Because of Winn-Dixie
by Kate DiCamillo

Questions

1. What does Opal want to buy for Winn-Dixie in the pet shop?

   _____

2. After Otis rejects Opal's installment plan proposal, how does she suggest she pay for the leash?

   _____

3. Who did Otis say that Gertrude the parrot was named after?

   _____

4. Give one example of how Gertrude was an amazing bird.

   _____

5. What unusual habit did Sweetie Pie Thomas have?

   _____

6. What did Sweetie Pie Thomas do that made Opal feel good?

   _____

Language Activity

Find **three** examples of the following **parts of speech** from this chapter.

Nouns	Verbs	Adjectives

Because of Winn-Dixie
by Kate DiCamillo

Chapters Nine and Ten

Before you read the chapters:

Have you ever formed an **unfavorable first impression** of someone because of their age or appearance, then discovered you were completely wrong? Write about such an experience, either real or imagined.

_____

_____

Vocabulary:

The words in the following list can be found in the word search. Circle each one in the puzzle and put a check mark beside the word in the list.

explained	Dewberry	Gertrude	trust	dessert
probably	preacher	notice	vegetables	introduced
amazed	whispered	grocery	Dunlap	invite
garden	false	careful	holler	instance

```
A  D  E  C  U  D  O  R  T  N  I  S  F  G  P
B  E  X  P  L  A  I  N  E  D  D  D  H  R  D
N  W  S  E  L  B  A  T  E  G  E  V  O  O  S
G  B  W  Q  C  A  R  E  F  U  L  B  L  C  A
E  E  T  R  E  S  S  E  D  F  A  A  L  E  G
C  R  R  E  S  L  A  F  H  B  F  V  E  R  A
N  R  U  T  C  V  N  N  L  C  G  H  R  Y  R
A  Y  S  A  R  B  N  Y  G  P  A  L  N  U  D
T  H  T  Z  X  U  I  N  V  I  T  E  G  H  E
S  A  M  A  Z  E  D  N  B  D  F  G  R  J  N
N  E  N  O  T  I  C  E  S  D  F  H  U  P  K
I  R  E  D  E  R  E  P  S  I  H  W  N  M  L
```

Because of Winn-Dixie
by Kate DiCamillo

Questions

1. To whom does Opal attribute all that happened to her that summer?

   _____

2. Why did Dunlap and Stevie Dewberry's mother shave their heads?

   _____

3. Why was Opal reluctant to go into the yard after Winn-Dixie?

   _____

4. Describe three things about Gloria Dump's appearance.

   _____

5. Why do you think Opal felt so free to speak to Gloria Dump about so many things?

   _____

6. What did Gloria Dump suspect Opal had also inherited from her mother?

   _____

Language Activity

The preacher was able to tell Opal ten things about her mother without too much **trouble. From what you have learned about Gloria Dump** in these chapters, list **ten** interesting things about her, either from what she says or about her home and surroundings. You may include things about her appearance, personality, conversation, or from *reading between the lines.*

_____

_____

_____

_____

_____

_____

Because of Winn-Dixie
by Kate DiCamillo

Chapter Eleven

Before you read the chapter:

Fears are sometimes very difficult to explain or understand. List **three** things that really give you the willies.

_____

_____

_____

Vocabulary:

In each of the following sets of words, **underline** the word that does not belong. Then, write a sentence explaining why it does not fit.

1. wail   whimper   willful   whine

_____

_____

2. crawled   crept   grovel   cranked

_____

_____

3. terrorize   harass   forlorn   bully

_____

_____

4. confused   neglected   rattled   flustered

_____

_____

5. forgive   pardon   excuse   sulk

_____

_____

Because of Winn-Dixie
by Kate DiCamillo

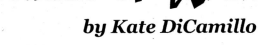

Questions

1. What was it that frightened Winn-Dixie?

   _____

2. Define "pathological fear".

   _____

3. Other than thunderstorms, what else might someone regard with a pathological fear?

   _____

4. What did the preacher mean when he said that after the thunderstorm, "the real Winn-Dixie will come back"?

   _____

5. What was unusual about the way that Winn-Dixie climbed up onto the couch after the storm?

   _____

6. Why didn't they want Winn-Dixie to get out during the storm?

   _____

7. What made Opal realize how much she loved the preacher at the end of the chapter?

   _____

Because of Winn-Dixie
by Kate DiCamillo

Language Activities

1. Choose any two **characters** you have already met in this novel. **Compare** four things about these two people. Consider such things as physical appearance, personality, age, and talents.

	Character 1 - _____	Character 2 - _____
1		
2		
3		
4		

2. Put the following words from chapter eleven in **alphabetical order**:

with   _____

Winn-Dixie   _____

whole   _____

whimpering   _____

would   _____

wrapped   _____

went   _____

was   _____

whining   _____

where   _____

Because of Winn-Dixie
by Kate DiCamillo

Chapter Twelve

Before you read the chapter:

People all over the world enjoy many different kinds of music (example: rock and roll). Name **three** other types (genres) of music.

_____

_____

What is your **favorite** type of music? Why?

_____

_____

Vocabulary:

Replace the words that are **underlined** in the sentences below with a word from the word list in the box. Remember to consider the context of the word in the sentence, as some words have several meanings.

counter	be quiet	probably	charming
slithering	exhaled	confused	criminal

1. The snake was **gliding** along the path to the campsite. _____

2. Charlie thought his team would **most likely** win the trophy. _____

3. The **felon** was sentenced by the judge to ten years in prison. _____

4. Sadie was **addled** when she first stepped from the roller coaster. _____

5. The actress was an **alluring** public figure. _____

6. Janet's mother told her to **keep still**. _____

7. The toolmaker laid the pliers on the **workbench**. _____

8. My fairy godmother **sighed** impatiently at my protests. _____

Because of Winn-Dixie

by Kate DiCamillo

Questions

1. What was unusual about the sight that greeted Opal when she visited the pet shop at the beginning of chapter twelve?

   _____

2. What "broke the spell" cast by Otis and his guitar?

   _____

3. What was faulty about Otis and Opal's original strategy in collecting the animals?

   _____

4. Describe the strategy suggested by Opal that was finally successful in collecting the animals.

   _____

5. What was to be the theme of Sweetie Pie's party?

   _____

6. How did Opal's mother like to laugh?

   _____

Language Activity

You have already met a number of fascinating characters in this novel. For each of the characters listed below, come up with three appropriate **adjectives** that would accurately describe them. Be sure to consider the character's **personality** as well as **appearance**! On the back of this sheet, make a chart like the one below, to fill in your answers.

Character	Trait One	Trait Two	Trait Three
Opal The Preacher Gloria Dump Franny Block Otis Dunlap Dewberry			

Because of Winn-Dixie
by Kate DiCamillo

Chapters Thirteen and Fourteen

Before you read the chapters:

Why do you think people put down other people and **call them names**? Do you think this can be harmful? Explain.

_____

_____

When meeting a person for the first time, what is a "**first impression**"? Explain how first impressions can be dangerous.

_____

_____

Vocabulary:

Using words from chapters thirteen and fourteen, complete the following crossword puzzle.

Across

3. to copy
4. rude
6. unusual
9. where a store's merchandise is placed
10. a part of the neck
13. What one does with a broom.
14. not smart
15. Stevie's brother
17. performances by musicians
19. the younger Dewberry brother
20. Franny's surname
22. short for professional development
23. a grown up
25. to read carefully or to ponder
26. a glass container
27. the organ we use to see with

Down

1. a woman who practices sorcery
2. move briskly from side to side
3. not a him or a her
5. Opal bought a red leather _____.
7. Gloria's last name
8. standard procedure
10. the gait of a horse
11. mentally slow
12. the Herman W. Block Library
15. Dunlap and Stevie's last name
16. Winn-Dixie was Opal's _____ dog.
18. Opal's little friend, _____ Pie
21. He owned Gertrude's Pets.
22. Opal and Gloria hosted one of these.
24. not night

Because of Winn-Dixie
by Kate DiCamillo

Questions

1. Why did Opal arrange the shelves at the pet shop instead of Otis?

_____

2. Where was Opal's favorite place to be that summer?

_____

3. Why do you think the Dewberry boys teased Opal and said mean things about Otis and Gloria Dump?

_____

4. According to Gloria, why were the Dewberry boys treating Opal the way they were?

_____

5. What was special about the tree in Gloria's backyard?

_____

6. Why do you think Gloria kept such a tree?

_____

7. Gloria's advice was that we should not "judge people by the things they done, but by what they are doing now." Do you agree or disagree with this advice? Explain.

_____

Language Activities

1. Alliteration is a literary device where the same consonants (usually at the beginning of words) are repeated. An example from this chapter is "**big bald-headed baby**".

   Use alliteration (**at least three additional words**) to describe the following items:

   a) party - _____

   _____

   b) dog - _____

   _____

   c) toffee - _____

   _____

2. Opal seems to have a good grasp on her **strengths** and **talents**. In chapter thirteen, she implies that she has an "eye for arranging things"; earlier in the book Gloria suggests that she inherited her mother's "green thumb". List **three** strengths or talents that you feel you have, then say whether or not you think Opal shares this talent or strength with you.

   _____

   _____

   _____

Because of Winn-Dixie
by Kate DiCamillo

Chapters Fifteen and Sixteen

Before you read the chapters:

Chapter fifteen reveals that Miss Franny is subject to "small fits". These are probably epileptic seizures. **Investigate** this illness and research a couple of points describing **epilepsy**.

_____

_____

Miss Franny makes the statement, "**war is hell**". Describe what you think this means.

_____

_____

Vocabulary:

A synonym is a word or word phrase that means the same as another. For example:

old = ancient	brave = courageous	beautiful = gorgeous

Below are partial sentences taken from chapters fifteen and sixteen. Replace the **underlined** words in each sentence with a synonym. Use a dictionary or a thesaurus to find your words. Place the new word on the blank after the phrase.

1. "Winn-Dixie . . . **hogged** it all." _____

2. "I held on to him and **comforted** him . . ." _____

3. ". . . those ghosts **chattering** . . . " _____

4. "Amanda sighed a real big **dramatic** sigh . . ." _____

5. "I **stole a look** at her." _____

6. "They have this abiding **notion** that war is fun." _____

7. ". . . when the firing on Fort Sumter **occurred**." _____

Because of Winn-Dixie
by Kate DiCamillo

8. "Artley W. Block had already **enlisted** . . ." _____

9. "Do you have any **suggestions**?" _____

10. "And no history lesson will **convince** them differently." _____

Questions

1. What annoying thing did Winn-Dixie do at the library?

   _____

2. What health problem did Miss Franny have? What is the proper medical term for this problem?

   _____

3. How did Winn-Dixie react to Miss Franny's problem?

   _____

4. What made Opal think of Gloria Dump when Miss Franny was having these problems?

   _____

5. What did Opal feel was the best way to comfort Gloria Dump?

   _____

6. Who came into the library just as Miss Franny began her story about the Civil War? What attitude did their visitor have?

   _____

7. According to Miss Franny, what abiding notion do men and boys have about war?

   _____

8. List three things about the war that were difficult for Miss Franny's great grandfather.

   _____

Because of Winn-Dixie
by Kate DiCamillo

9. What would have become of Miss Fanny if Littmus Block had been killed in the war?

_____

10. What happened to Littmus' family while he was away at the war?

_____

Language Activities

1. Franny Block tells Opal a number of interesting things about the **American Civil War** in these chapters. Choose **one** of the following items from the selection below and write a sentence or two telling about how it played a part in either Miss Franny's story or the American Civil War.

typhoid fever slavery	Yankee states' rights	Gone with the Wind fleas and lice

_____

_____

_____

_____

_____

_____

2. Do you agree or disagree with the following statement: "'**War**', said Miss Franny with her eyes still closed, '**should be a cuss word too**.'" Explain what you think Miss Franny meant by her comment and why she felt that way. Do you think war is ever necessary? Write your answer on a separate sheet of paper.

3. On a separate sheet of paper, write a **letter to the local newspaper editor** giving your opinion on the subject of whether war is necessary. Defend your point of view by including details as to why it should or should not be a part of life today.

Because of Winn-Dixie
by Kate DiCamillo

Chapter Seventeen

Before you read the chapter:

What is your favourite **candy**? Describe how it tastes. How does it make you feel when you eat this candy?

_____

_____

Vocabulary:

Circle the word that matches the meaning of the **underlined** word in the sentence.

1. The most important **ingredient** in the punch was ginger ale.

    a) force   **b)** lunch   **c)** part   **d)** liquid

2. The Littmus Lozenges were **manufactured** in Florida.

    a) made   **b)** sugared   **c)** sold   **d)** grown

3. Opal had a strange **sensation** in the pit of her stomach.

    a) rumbling   **b)** hollow   **c)** discoloring   **d)** feeling

4. Otis had to **concentrate** very hard before answering.

    a) argue   **b)** think   **c)** speak   **d)** push

5. Gloria Dump **figured** it was the perfect night for a party.

    a) bragged   **b)** argued   **c)** thought   **d)** doubted

6. Stevie Dewberry was **especially** mean to Opal.

    a) particularly   **b)** terribly   **c)** not   **d)** stupidly

7. Making **decisions** was particularly difficult for Otis.

    a) music   **b)** choices   **c)** arguments   **d)** friends

8. By suppertime, Opal had worked up a real **appetite**.

   a) crying fit   **b)** floor show   **c)** argument   **d)** hunger

9. Gertrude was the most **famous** parrot in town.

   a) well-known   **b)** annoying   **c)** mouthy   **d)** polite

10. The lozenges made the Block family **fortune**.

    a) famous   **b)** depressed   **c)** riches   **d)** fabulous

Questions

1. After crying for his lost family, what strange sensation did Littmus have?

   _____

2. What did Littmus plan while he was walking to Florida?

   _____

3. What two flavors did the Littmus Lozenge taste like?

   _____   _____

4. How did it make Opal feel when she ate the candy?

   _____

5. What secret ingredient did the Littmus Lozenge contain?

   _____

6. What was Opal's biggest sadness?

   _____

7. Who did it remind Amanda of?

   _____

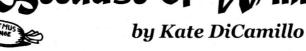
Because of Winn-Dixie
by Kate DiCamillo

8. Why did Opal decide to wave at the Dewberry boys instead of sticking out her tongue at them?

_____

Language Activities

1. A **compound word** is composed of two or more words united together. For example, **some + where = somewhere**. In the following activity, one word from column A must be joined to the word in column B.

Column A	Column B	Compound Word
battle	room	
some	telling	
any	way	
story	storms	
back	nut	
birth	light	
thunder	field	
pea	day	
bed	yard	
flash	thing	

Because of Winn-Dixie
by Kate DiCamillo

2. You have been introduced to a number of very interesting characters and places in **Naomi, Florida**. The author doesn't really tell us much about the layout of the town, so you will have to use your imagination to complete this assignment!

Sketch and label a map of Naomi as you imagine it. Be sure to include the following places:

- Opal and the preacher's trailer
- the library
- the pet shop

- Gloria Dump's house
- Dunlap and Stevie's house
- the church

Because of Winn-Dixie
by Kate DiCamillo

Chapter Eighteen

Before you read the chapter:

Were you ever forced to **apologize** for something you did not do? How would this make you feel? Why?

_____

_____

How can **idle conversation** be harmful? Can you think of an example of how it might be destructive?

_____

_____

Vocabulary:

Analogies are equations in which the first pair of words has the same relationship as the second pair of words. For example, **stop** is to **go** as **fast** is to **slow**. Both pairs of words are opposites. Choose the best word from the word box to complete each of the analogies below.

separate	conversation	tragedies	mention	melancholy
important	supposed	surprising	peculiar	suffered

1. Late is to **tardy** as **odd** is to _____.

2. Hot is to **cold** as **comedies** is to _____.

3. Red is to **crimson** as **sad** is to _____.

4. Shallow is to **deep** as **insignificant** is to _____.

5. Beautiful is to **ugly** as **unite** is to _____.

6. Smooth is to **rough** as **enjoyed** is to _____.

7. Ill-mannered is to **rude** as **cite** is to _____.

8. Pale is to **ashen** as **imagined** is to _____.

9. Safe is to **dangerous** as **predictable** is to _____.

10. Book is to **text** as **communication** is to _____.

Questions

1. What did the taste of the Littmus Lozenge remind Gloria Dump of?

    _____

2. Why did Opal read the book in a loud voice?

    _____

3. The Littmus Lozenge made the preacher think of which person?

    _____

4. What complaint had been made to the preacher about Opal?

    _____

5. What did the preacher think Opal should do about the complaint?

    _____

6. Who was Carson, and what happened to him?

    _____

7. How did this help Opal to understand Amanda better?

    _____

Because of Winn-Dixie

by Kate DiCamillo

Language Activities

1. A **triangle poem** has five lines and gets its name from the shape of the poem.

   This is the pattern: **Line 1 – Title**
   Line 2 – Two **touch** words
   Line 3 – Three **sound** words
   Line 4 – Four **sight** words
   Line 5 – Five **taste** words
   } Lines 2 to 5 all refer to the title.

   On a separate sheet of paper, write a triangle poem about the Littmus Lozenge.

2. An **anagram** is a word that is formed by changing the order of the letters of another word. For example, the letters in the word **was** can also form the word **saw**.

   Follow the directions below to form the anagrams:

   a) Read the clue in the right-hand column.

   b) Make an anagram using the word in the left-hand column; move the letters around in any order but you must use all the letters.

Word	Anagram	Clue
past		two are in your kitchen sink
treads		she looked hard at someone
dear		something you do with a book
war		not cooked
sad		short for advertisements
seven		opposite of odds
aids		spoken
dogs		idols

Because of Winn-Dixie
by Kate DiCamillo

Chapter Nineteen

Before you read the chapter:

Injustice. What does this word mean? Can you think of an example to demonstrate this concept?

_____

_____

Vocabulary:

Read each of the sentences below. Define, in your own words, what you think each word means. Then find out what the word really means.

1. The convict was a very **dangerous** man.
2. The police put him in **handcuffs**.
3. The **lozenge** was most delicious.
4. Opal lost her **nerve** when she faced the angry dog.
5. The directions to Grandmother's house were very **confusing**.
6. The teacher decided to **separate** the twins.
7. The preacher asked Opal to **apologize**.
8. The elm tree was killed by a rare **disease**.

Word	Guess	Real Meaning
dangerous		
handcuffs		
lozenge		
nerve		
confusing		
separate		
apologize		
disease		

Because of Winn-Dixie
by Kate DiCamillo

Questions

1. What did Otis ask Opal after she gave him the candy?

   _____

2. What did the taste of the candy remind Otis of?

   _____

3. Why had Otis been put in jail?

   _____

4. What did they make Otis promise after releasing him from jail?

   _____

5. How did Sweetie Pie react to the candy? What did it taste like to her?

   _____

6. Why did Opal sweep the floor "real slow" that day?

   _____

Language Activities

1. Write the number of **syllables** found in each of the words from this chapter.

Littmus	_____	sometimes	_____	Gertrude	_____
thank	_____	empty	_____	company	_____
mouth	_____	said	_____	spit	_____
better	_____	promise	_____	Halloween	_____
scream	_____	dangerous	_____	police	_____

2. Interview at least **three** other students for their views of this novel so far. Try to get both positive and negative comments. Write a brief report putting these views together on a separate sheet of paper.

Because of Winn-Dixie

by Kate DiCamillo

Chapter Twenty

Before you read the chapter:

Parties can be a lot of fun. What do you think are four **essential ingredients** in any successful party?

_____   _____

_____   _____

Describe a party you attended (or would like to attend) that was a lot of fun. Why was it so much fun?

_____

_____

Vocabulary:

Choose a word from the word bank to complete each definition:

criminal library	idea whisper	elbow dangerous	squeeze barbecue	triangle promise

1. An outdoor grill for roasting meat is a _____.

2. To speak in a very quiet voice is to _____.

3. An oath is a _____.

4. A building where books are kept for loan is a _____.

5. To apply pressure with your hand is to _____.

6. A three-sided figure is a _____.

7. An outlaw or felon is a _____.

8. The opposite of safe is _____.

9. A creative thought is an _____.

10. A body part is the _____.

Because of Winn-Dixie
by Kate DiCamillo

Questions

1. What do you think Gloria Dump meant when she said "sometimes things are so sad they get to be funny"?

   _____

2. Where did Opal get the idea to have a party?

   _____

3. According to Opal, what kind of sandwiches do adults like?

   _____

4. Who did Gloria insist that Opal invite to the party?

   _____

5. What response did Opal expect when she asked Amanda to the party?

   _____

6. What did Stevie expect Gloria Dump to do to him if he attended the party at her place?

   _____

7. What question did Sweetie Pie ask when Opal invited her to the party? What was Sweetie Pie's suggestion in this regard?

   _____

8. What did Opal promise to do if Otis came to her party?

   _____

Because of Winn-Dixie
by Kate DiCamillo

Language Activities

1. Missing People

What do you think of Opal's statement, "Do you think everybody misses somebody? Like I miss my mama?" Gloria seems to agree with her when she says, "I believe, sometimes that the whole world has an aching heart." Do you think Opal is right that everybody misses somebody? Is it true in your own life?

_____

_____

_____

_____

_____

_____

_____

2. Antonyms, Synonyms or Homonyms

Beside each pair of words write **A** (antonym) or **S** (synonym) or **H** (homonym).

a) for – four _____

b) to – two _____

c) allowed – aloud _____

d) see – sea _____

e) smiled - grinned _____

f) preacher - minister _____

g) excited - bored _____

h) quick - slow _____

i) lovely - wonderful _____

j) back - front _____

Because of Winn-Dixie
by Kate DiCamillo

Chapters Twenty-One and Twenty-Two

Before you read the chapters:

A wise man once said, "Don't ever say, 'Oh well, at least things can't get any worse' – because they probably will!" Do you **agree** with this statement? Explain. Can you think of an incident from your own experiences to support or disprove this statement?

_____

_____

_____

Vocabulary:

Draw a straight line to connect the vocabulary word to its definition. Remember to use a straight edge.

1.	desperate	make someone laugh
2.	crepe	delight
3.	convince	unhopeful
4.	predict	be thankful for
5.	probably	foretell
6.	shimmery	considerate
7.	appreciate	ensure
8.	amuse	type of paper
9.	polite	glimmering
10.	pleasure	most likely

Because of Winn-Dixie

by Kate DiCamillo

Questions

1. Why did Opal and Gloria decide to have their party at night?

   _____

2. What were the three ingredients of *Dump Punch*?

   _____

3. Why did Sweetie Pie bring pictures of dogs to the party?

   _____

4. What did Otis bring to the party?

   _____

5. What task did they give the preacher at the party?

   _____

6. What happened at the end of chapter twenty-two that disrupted the party?

   _____

Because of Winn-Dixie

by Kate DiCamillo

Language Activity

Although Opal and Gloria did not advertise for their party, and only invited their friends, imagine that they decided to invite the people of their neighborhood. Create and design a brochure advertising Opal and Gloria Dump's party. Be sure to include an appropriate picture (perhaps with party decorations) as well as a catchy slogan that would be sure to draw the people of the neighborhood. Use the template below to plan and sketch your brochure.

Outside Pages

Back Cover   Front Cover

Inside Pages

Inside Left Page   Inside Right Page

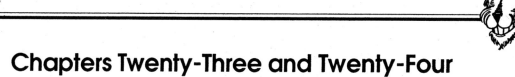

Because of Winn-Dixie
by Kate DiCamillo

Chapters Twenty-Three and Twenty-Four

Before you read the chapters:

Friendship: What is a friend? Describe a personal incident when a friend stuck by you during a difficult time. How did this make you feel?

_____

_____

_____

Vocabulary:

1. Antonyms are words with opposite meanings. Draw a line from each word in column A to its antonym in column B. Then, use the words in column A to fill in the blanks in the sentences below.

A	B
a) protect	above
b) believe	misunderstands
c) underneath	agree
d) argue	attack
e) realizes	know

2. a) The motto of the police is to serve and _____.

   b) When Sally was a little girl, she used to _____ in Santa Claus.

   c) No one was sure what lay _____ the streets of the city.

   d) "Don't _____ with me all the time," his mother said.

   e) Everyone now _____ what a great hockey player Wayne Gretzky was.

 # Because of Winn-Dixie
by Kate DiCamillo

Questions

1. What had Opal forgotten about when the thunderstorm began?

   _____

2. Do you agree with Gloria's statement, "You can only love what you got while you got it?"

   _____

3. Why did Sweetie Pie think that Winn-Dixie was not lost?

   _____

4. What was Opal afraid might have happened to Winn-Dixie?

   _____

5. What did Opal think about in order to take her mind off losing Winn-Dixie?

   _____

6. Who urged Opal to give up looking for Winn-Dixie in the rain? What was her reaction to this suggestion?

   _____

7. What else did Opal accuse her father of "giving up on"?

   _____

8. Why do you think the preacher cried in chapter twenty-four?

   _____

9. What important thing had Opal's mother left behind when she left home?

   _____

Because of Winn-Dixie
by Kate DiCamillo

Language Activities

1. The Lost Pet

Have you ever experienced losing a pet as Opal did? How would such an experience make you feel?

_____

_____

_____

_____

_____

2. Root Words

Beside each word from these chapters, write its **root word**:

a) grabbed _____   **b)** finally _____

c) shouting _____   **d)** wrapped _____

e) probably _____   **f)** whistling _____

g) glowing _____   **h)** thought _____

i) cried _____   **j)** tried _____

Because of Winn-Dixie
by Kate DiCamillo

Chapter Twenty-Five

Before you read the chapter:

Winn-Dixie is lost! **Predict** what you think will happen in the story before reading chapter twenty-five.

_____

_____

_____

_____

Vocabulary:

In each of the following sets of words, **underline** the one word which does not belong. Then, write a sentence explaining why it does not fit.

1. gratify   please   satisfy   disappointed

    _____

2. possible   unlikely   conceivable   plausible

    _____

3. convinced   uncertain   believing   confident

    _____

4. myth   legend   biography   saga

    _____

5. hymn   prose   psalm   poem

    _____

6. tendon   potion   dose   draught

    _____

Because of Winn-Dixie
by Kate DiCamillo

Questions

1. Describe what was going on back at Gloria Dump's house when Opal and the preacher returned.

   _____

2. Where was Winn-Dixie all along? How did he give himself away to the others?

   _____

3. Why do you think Stevie Dewberry looked disappointed when he admitted that Gloria wasn't a witch?

   _____

4. Why did Winn-Dixie look like a ghost when they found him?

   _____

5. What kind of a "gift" did Gloria say that Otis had?

   _____

Because of Winn-Dixie
by Kate DiCamillo

Language Activities

1. Conflict is an important element in a novel. There are generally three types of conflict: **person against person**; **person against self**; and **person against nature**. *Choose one of these types of conflicts and find an example of it in Because of Winn-Dixie.*

   _____
   _____
   _____
   _____

2. **In Other Words**
   Put the following expressions from this chapter into your own words. If you're stuck, check the context of the quote.

   "He'd plumb wore out." _____

   "Them witchy things . . ." _____

   "He looked all lit up from the inside." _____

   "I felt my heart swell up inside me with pure happiness." _____

   _____

Because of Winn-Dixie
by Kate DiCamillo

Chapter Twenty-Six

Before you read the chapter:

Of all the new friends that Opal makes in this novel, which one did you like the **best**? Why?

_____

_____

Did Winn-Dixie **play a part** in Opal making friends with this particular person? Explain.

_____

_____

Vocabulary:

Choose a word from the list that means the same or nearly the same as the **underlined** word.

constellations	unwrapped	echoed	twigs
teasing	planets	below	strummed

1. Otis **picked** the strings of his guitar. _____

2. Opal examined the **groups of stars** in the night sky. _____

3. John was **pestering** his sister. _____

4. The presents were **underneath** the Christmas tree. _____

5. The earth is one of nine **spheres**. _____

6. Ralphie **opened** one of his birthday gifts early. _____

7. Many of the old maple's **branches** were broken in the ice storm. _____

8. The prospector's voice **reverberated** in the canyon. _____

Because of Winn-Dixie

by Kate DiCamillo

Questions

Beside each of the following quotations from this chapter, write the name of the correct speaker.

Stevie Dunlap	Miss Franny Otis	Sweetie Pie Amanda	Opal The Preacher

1. "I know ten things about you, and that's not enough." _____

2. "Are you praying?" _____

3. "You shouldn't be running around in the dark." _____

4. "Are you here to sing some songs with us?" _____

5. "Care for a Littmus Lozenge?" _____

6. "Do you want a pickle?" _____

7. "Yeah, are we gonna sing or what?" _____

8. "Let's sing for the dog." _____

Language Activities

1. Do you think it's a good idea for someone to have **a mistake tree** like Gloria did? What would be the purpose of such a tree? How might it help a person like Gloria?

   _____

   _____

   _____

   _____

   _____

   _____

Because of Winn-Dixie
by Kate DiCamillo

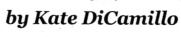

2. Create a **time line** for *Because of Winn-Dixie* indicating the **ten** most important events of the novel and the order in which they happened.

3. Design a **book cover** for *Because of Winn-Dixie*. Be sure to include the title, author's name, and an interesting picture. Make sure that your work is neat and careful, and that you color your creation. Use the template below to plan your book cover.

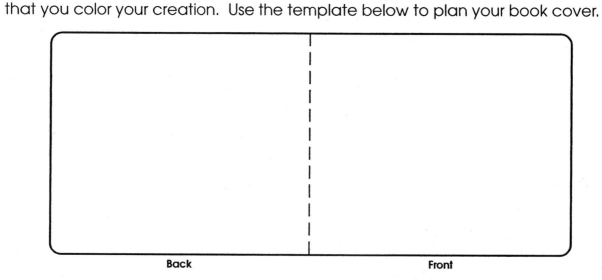

Back   Front

Because of Winn-Dixie
by Kate DiCamillo

Answer Key

Chapters One and Two: *(page 11)*
Vocabulary:

1. immediately   2. distracted   3. sermon   4. concerned   5. display
6. exceptions   7. cashier   8. admit   9. specific   10. hollered

Questions:

1. big, tongue hanging out, wagging tail, skinny, bald patches, ugly
2. The corners of his mouth pulled up.
3. macaroni-and-cheese, white rice and two tomatoes
4. a dog
5. The dog would be killed.
6. It was so unkept-looking.
7. summer in Naomi, Florida
8. Missionary in India – answers may vary
9. sermons, prayers and suffering people
10. Answers may vary (he probably felt sorry for the dog).

Chapters Three and Four: *(page 14)*
Vocabulary:

1. e   2. h   3. i   4. g   5. a   6. b   7. j   8. f   9. c   10. d

Questions:

1. The dog really tensed up and looked insulted (didn't show his teeth or wag his tail).
2. She heard the ladies at the church in Watley talking about him.
3. She left her friends in Watley when they moved to Naomi.
4. Answers may vary (she was lonely).
5. She was afraid he would get mad at her.
6. He started sneezing.

Chapter Five: *(page 16)*
Vocabulary: Answers may vary.

Questions:

1. He made a mess – howled
2. One of: used to be a Pick-It-Quick store, no pews, people brought foldup chairs, quite informal
3. He was howling.
4. He caught a mouse and dropped it at the preacher's feet.
5. He suggested they pray for the mouse.
6. Opal thought the other children would think she would tell on them to the preacher and they would get into trouble with their parents and God.

Chapters Six and Seven: *(page 18)*
Vocabulary:

1. unusual   2. conscious   3. correctly   4. rear   5. choose   6. arrogant   7. meant

Questions:

1. She thought Winn-Dixie was a bear.
2. When a bear came into her library.
3. a library
4. *War and Peace*
5. She was very proud – she said "I am an advanced reader".

Chapter Eight: *(page 20)*
Vocabulary: Answers may vary.

Questions:

1. a leash and collar
2. She would come in and sweep the floor and dust the shelves and take out the trash until it's paid off.
3. the owner of the pet shop
4. Answers may vary (she can speak, she can identify a dog, she sat on Winn-Dixie's head).
5. Sucking the knuckle of her third finger.
6. She invited Opal to a party.

Chapters Nine and Ten: *(page 22)*

Vocabulary:

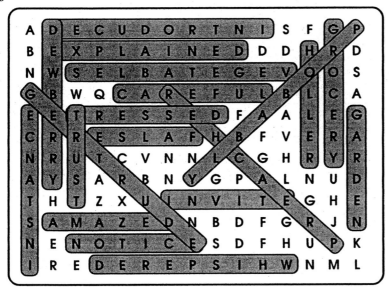

Questions:
1. Winn-Dixie
2. One time Dunlap got fleas in his hair from their cat.
3. The boys told her the house belonged to a witch.
4. old with crinkly brown skin, wore a big floppy hat, didn't have any teeth
5. Answers may vary (she was an adult; she didn't go to Opal's church; she was accepting of what Opal said).
6. her green thumb

Chapter Eleven: *(page 24)*

Vocabulary:
1. willful – the other words are all sounds
2. cranked – the other words are all movements
3. forlorn – the other words are all synonyms of bully
4. neglected – the other words all mean confused
5. sulk – the other words all mean forgive

Questions:
1. the thunder and lightning
2. A fear that goes way beyond normal fears. It's a fear you can't be talked out of or reasoned out of.
3. Answers may vary (i.e., spiders, snakes, water, closed spaces, heights).
4. He will be back to the way he was before the storm.
5. He kept kind of sliding himself onto the couch, looking off in a different direction, like it's all happening by accident.
6. He might run away and not come back.
7. for forgiving Winn-Dixie and trying to keep him safe

Language Activities:
Alphabetical order: was, went, where, whimpering, whining, whole, Winn-Dixie, with, would, wrapped

Chapter Twelve: *(page 27)*

Vocabulary:
1. slithering   2. probably   3. criminal   4. confused   5. charming   6. be quiet
7. counter   8. exhaled

Questions:
1. All the animals were out of their cages and were peacefully gathered around Otis, who was playing his guitar in the middle of the store.

2. Gertrude croaked "dog" and flew over and landed on Winn-Dixie's head. Then Otis stopped playing the guitar and the spell was broken.
3. Otis and Opal kept bumping into each other and tripping over the animals.
4. Opal got Otis to play his guitar. Then all the animals sat still and they were able to gather them up.
5. pink
6. She liked to laugh out loud.

Chapters Thirteen and Fourteen: *(page 29)*

Vocabulary:

```
W          W  I  M  I  T  A  T  E
I  G  N  O  R  A  N  T
T        G        L     O  D  D
C     R     S  H  E  L  V  E  S     U
T  H  R  O  A  T        A     R     M
R     U              M  S  W  E  E  P
O  S  T  U  P  I  D     E     H     T
T     I              M        A
D  U  N  L  A  P  C  O  N  C  E  R  T  S
E     E        R           D     W
W     S  T  E  V  I  E           E
B  L  O  C  K        A     P  D
E  T     A  D  U  L  T     A
R  I     A              R        I
R  S  T  U  D  Y     B  O  T  T  L  E
E  Y  E              Y
```

Questions:
1. Otis didn't have an eye for arranging things.
2. the Herman W. Block Memorial Library
3. Answers may vary.
4. She thought they just wanted to be friends with Opal in a roundabout way.
5. The tree had a lot of bottles hanging from it.
6. Perhaps to remind her of the struggles from her past.
7. Answers may vary.

Chapters Fifteen and Sixteen: *(page 32)*

Vocabulary: Answers may vary.

Questions:
1. He hogged the fan.
2. She had small fits – probably epileptic seizures.
3. He would go over and sit by Miss Franny's side as if protecting her.
4. Opal wondered who comforted Gloria when she heard the bottles knocking together and was reminded about all the things she had done wrong.
5. to read her a book loud enough to keep the ghosts from her past away
6. Amanda Wilkinson – she pretended she wasn't interested in Opal and in what she and Miss Franny were doing.
7. that war is fun
8. Three of : hunger, fleas and lice, cold in the winter and hot in the summer, getting shot at, stinking, itchy
9. She wouldn't have existed.
10. Everyone else died and their house was burned down.

Chapter Seventeen: *(page 35)*

Vocabulary:
1. part
2. made
3. feeling
4. think
5. thought
6. particularly
7. choices
8. hunger
9. well-known
10. riches

Questions:
1. He felt like he wanted something sweet.
2. He was planning the candy factory.
3. root beer and strawberry
4. It made her think of things she felt sad about.
5. sorrow
6. Her mother left her when she was small.
7. It made her miss Carson.
8. Opal thought about what Miss Franny had said about war being hell, and that Gloria had told her not to judge the boys too hard.

Language Activities:
battlefield, something, anyway, storytelling, backyard, birthday, thunderstorms, peanut, bedroom, flashlight

Chapter Eighteen: *(page 39)*
Vocabulary:
1. peculiar
2. tragedies
3. melancholy
4. important
5. separate
6. suffered
7. mention
8. supposed
9. surprising
10. conversation

Questions:
1. like people leaving
2. to keep her ghosts away
3. Opal's mother
4. Mrs. Dewberry told the preacher that Opal had called Stevie a bald-headed baby.
5. apologize
6. Carson was Amanda's five-year-old brother who drowned the previous year.
7. It helped Opal understand why Amanda was so pinch-faced.

Language Activities:
Anagrams: taps, stared, read, raw, ads, evens, said, gods

Chapter Nineteen: *(page 42)*
Vocabulary: Answers may vary.

Questions:
1. Is it Halloween?
2. being in jail
3. He was playing his guitar on the street and wouldn't stop when the police asked him to. He then hit a policeman.
4. never to play his guitar on the street again
5. She spit it out because it tasted like not having a dog.
6. To keep Otis company because she realized he was lonely.

Language Activities:
1. littmus - 2   sometimes - 2   Gertrude - 2   thank - 1   empty - 2   company - 3
   mouth - 1   said - 1   spit - 1   better - 2   promise - 2 Halloween - 3
   scream - 1   dangerous - 3   police - 2

Chapter Twenty: *(page 44)*
Vocabulary:
1. barbeque
2. whisper
3. promise
4. library
5. squeeze
6. triangle
7. criminal
8. dangerous
9. idea
10. elbow

Questions:
1. Answers may vary.
2. from the barbecue scene in *Gone With the Wind*.
3. egg salad
4. the Dewberry brothers
5. a rejection
6. She might cook them up in her big old witch's pot.
7. What's the theme? - dogs

8. clean the pet shop free for a week

Language Activities:
  2. a) H   **b)** H   **c)** H   **d)** H   **e)** S   **f)** S   **g)** A   **h)** A   **i)** S   **j)** A

Chapters Twenty-One and Twenty Two: *(page 47)*
Vocabulary:
  1. unhopeful   **2.** type of paper   **3.** ensure   **4.** foretell   **5.** most likely
  6. glimmering   **7.** be thankful for   **8.** make someone laugh   **9.** considerate   **10.** delight

Questions:
  1. It would be cooler.   **2.** orange juice, grapefruit juice, soda
  3. She wanted it to be a dog theme.   **4.** a big jar of pickles
  5. to say grace   **6.** a rainstorm

Chapters Twenty-Three and Twenty-Four: *(page 50)*
Vocabulary:
  1. a) protect – attack   **b)** believe – know   **c)** underneath – above   **d)** argue – agree
    e) realizes – misunderstands
  2. a) protect   **b)** believe   **c)** underneath   **d)** argue   **e)** realizes

Questions:
  1. Winn-Dixie
  2. Answers may vary.
  3. The dog was too smart to get lost.
  4. She was afraid he'd run away and wouldn't come back - she was also afraid he might have been run over.
  5. She came up with ten things about Winn-Dixie she could put on a Lost Poster.
  6. the preacher - she wanted to keep looking and not give up
  7. her mother
  8. Answers may vary (grief over his lost wife – letting Opal down).
  9. Opal

Language Activities:
  1. a) grab   **b)** final   **c)** shout   **d)** wrap   **e)** probable
    f) whistle   **g)** glow   **h)** think   **i)** cry   **j)** try

Chapter Twenty-Five: *(page 53)*
Vocabulary:
  1. disappointed – all other words mean to *satisfy*
  2. unlikely – all other words mean *possible*
  3. uncertain – opposite of other words which all mean *convinced*
  4. biography – all other words relate to mythology
  5. prose – all other words are forms of poetry
  6. tendon – all other words have to do with a portion of something

Questions:
  1. They were all singing while Otis played his guitar.
  2. He had been hiding under Gloria's bed – he sneezed.
  3. The idea of her being a witch was more exciting.
  4. He was covered in dust.
  5. Otis was able to pick out tunes on his guitar right quick.

Chapter Twenty-Six: *(page 56)*
Vocabulary:
  1. strummed   **2.** constellations   **3.** teasing   **4.** below   **5.** planets   **6.** unwrapped
  7. twigs   **8.** echoed

Questions:
  1. Opal   **2.** Dunlap   **3.** Amanda   **4.** the preacher   **5.** Miss Franny   **6.** Otis
  7. Stevie   **8.** Sweetie Pie